I Know Someone with
Down's Syndrome

Vic Parker

www.raintreepublishers.co.uk
Visit our website to find out
more information about
Raintree books.

To order:
☎ Phone 0845 6044371
▤ Fax +44 (0) 1865 312263
▥ Email myorders@raintreepublishers.co.uk

Customers from outside the UK please telephone +44 1865 312262

Raintree is an imprint of Capstone Global Library
Limited, a company incorporated in England and
Wales having its registered office at 7 Pilgrim Street,
London, EC4V 6LB – Registered company number:
6695582

Text © Capstone Global Library Limited 2011
First published in hardback in 2011
The moral rights of the proprietor have been asserted.

Edited by Rebecca Rissman, Daniel Nunn
  and Siân Smith
Designed by Joanna Hinton Malivoire
Picture research by Mica Brancic
Originated by Capstone Global Library
Printed and bound in China by Leo Paper Products Ltd

ISBN 978 1 406 22077 3
15 14 13 12 11
10 9 8 7 6 5 4 3 2 1

British Library Cataloguing in Publication Data
Parker, Victoria.
I know someone with Down's syndrome. –
(Understanding health issues)
   1. Down syndrome–Juvenile literature.
   I. Title II. Series
   616.8'58842-dc22

Acknowledgements
We would like to thank the following for permission to
reproduce photographs: Alamy p. 15 (© Steve Skjold);
Corbis pp. 12 (Design Pics/© Leah Warkentin), 21, 22
(© Mika), 25 (© Gabe Palmer); Getty Images pp. 5
(Aurora/Rhea Anna), 9 (Stockbyte/George Doyle), 18
(Realistic Reflections), 23 (Designs pics); Karen Gaffney
p. 27; © Newspix p. 15 (News Ltd/Peter Clark); PA p. 14
(John Birdsall/John Birdsall); Photolibrary pp. 4 (Design
Pics Inc/Kristy-Anne Glubish), 8 (Moodboard), 10
(Corbis), 11 (Peter Arnold Images/Ed Reschke); Press
Association pp. 17 (EMPICS Sport/Nigel French), 20
(The Washington Time/Landov); Science Photo Library
pp. 6, 7 (JOTI), 13 (James King-Holmes); The Kobal
Collection p. 26 (Warner Bros TV).

Cover photograph of a girl with Down's syndrome
relaxing on snow after skiing reproduced with
permission of iStockphoto.com (© Diloute).

We would like to thank Matthew Siegel, Ashley Wolinski,
and Stuart Mills for their invaluable help in the
preparation of this book.

Contents

Some words are printed in bold, **like this**. You can
find out what they mean in the glossary.

Do you know someone with Down's syndrome?

You might have a friend with Down's syndrome. Down's syndrome is a **medical condition** that people are born with. It affects a person's body and their learning abilities, too.

Someone you know could have Down's syndrome.

Down's syndrome is not a disease and people who have it do not usually feel ill. They can live active, happy lives.

How does Down's syndrome affect people?

People with Down's syndrome are all different. It can take young children with Down's syndrome longer to learn some skills. These might include walking, talking, doing tricky tasks with their hands, reading, and remembering things.

Children with Down's syndrome may seem younger than other children of the same age.

Some people with Down's syndrome use **sign language** or pictures to help them explain what they mean.

If the effects of Down's syndrome are very strong then some people may not be able to learn some skills fully. They may need more help and to find other ways of doing things.

Some people with mild Down's syndrome are very good at different hobbies.

Other people are only mildly affected by Down's syndrome. They may learn to do certain skills, such as painting pictures, better than other people without Down's syndrome.

Many people with Down's syndrome go on to do exactly the same things that other people do. They can go to school and college, have jobs, and get married.

9

The cause of Down's syndrome

Our bodies are made up of millions of pieces too small to see, called **cells**. Every cell contains a tiny thread of information. This tells our bodies how to grow and **develop**.

You can see cells if you use a piece of equipment called a **microscope**.

People with Down's syndrome have extra bits of this thread of information in their cells. This tells their bodies to grow and develop in some different ways to the bodies of other people.

This is what a human body cell looks like through a microscope.

Who gets Down's syndrome?

Babies born with Down's syndrome can be smaller than other babies.

Any baby can have Down's syndrome, no matter what the race or nationality of their parents. Older mothers are more likely to have babies with Down's syndrome than younger mothers.

About 1 in every 800 to 1,000 babies born has Down's syndrome. If someone is born with Down's syndrome, it will never go away. If you are not born with it, you cannot get it later.

Many scientists are working to find out why some people are born with Down's syndrome.

At school

Some children with Down's syndrome go to special schools, where they can have expert help with learning. Everybody has different ways that they learn best.

Children at special schools have more one-to-one attention from teachers than at an ordinary school.

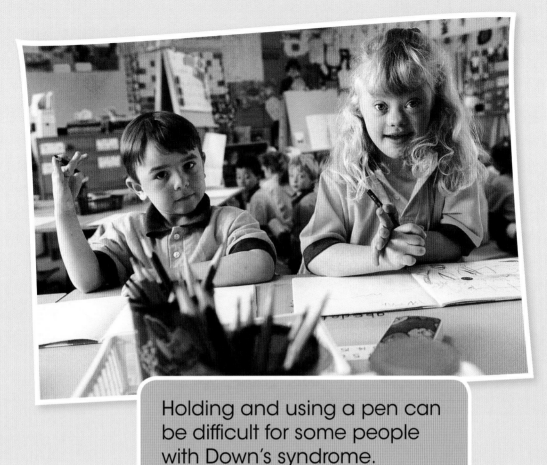

Holding and using a pen can be difficult for some people with Down's syndrome.

Many children with Down's syndrome go to ordinary schools. Some have assistants to help them. They may also have special classes for learning things they find harder.

At play

We can all learn new things through playing.

All children love to play, whether it is making things or imagining things. Many types of play can help children with Down's syndrome improve their **coordination** or movement skills.

Children with Down's syndrome often enjoy exercise, like dancing, or sports. Some take part with children without Down's syndrome, while others take part in competitions or teams especially for people with **disabilities**.

These football players with Down's Syndrome are playing in a tournament.

Spending time with others

Having good friends makes life fun.

Children with Down's syndrome have the same feelings as everyone else. If they are left out they will feel hurt and sad. So treat them the same as your other friends.

Children with Down's syndrome like joining in with everybody. We are all happier when we have friends around. People with Down's syndrome can be very caring, loyal friends.

Friends can share many great times together.

Health problems

A person with Down's syndrome can catch colds and coughs more often than someone else. They may also have problems with their sight, hearing, or how food passes through their body.

This girl with Down's syndrome wears a **hearing aid** to help with her hearing.

Many people with Down's syndrome wear glasses to help with their sight.

However, all these things can be helped with medical care, so they can live healthy lives. Some people with Down's syndrome do not have any health problems at all.

Growing older with Down's syndrome

People with Down's syndrome can grow up to make choices for themselves. They may choose to live in places where there are people to help them. They may be able to live on their own or with a partner, and go out to work.

Some adults with Down's syndrome have care assistants who sometimes help them.

People with Down's syndrome can live into their sixties or even longer.

People with Down's syndrome get older just like everyone else. Sometimes people get confused more easily or begin to forget things as they get old. This can happen earlier to people with Down's syndrome.

Being a good friend

There are many ways you can be a good friend to someone with Down's syndrome. Some of these are shown in the list below.

You can:

- play games that you both enjoy
- help them with tricky tasks but don't take over or do everything for them
- stick up for each other if you need to.

We all have different bodies and personalities.

Living with Down's syndrome can be difficult at times. We are all different in many ways. A good friend likes us and values us for who we are.

Famous people with Down's syndrome

American Luke Zimmerman has always loved acting. He once played the lead role in Shakespeare's play *Romeo and Juliet*. He is a student at a performing arts college, and appears on television regularly.

Luke Zimmerman stars in a programme called *The Secret Life of the American Teenager*.

Karen Gaffney enjoys all sorts of different swimming challenges.

Karen Gaffney is such a good swimmer that she swam in a six-person team across a sea, all the way from England to France. She has also studied at college to be a teaching assistant.

Down's syndrome – facts and fiction

Facts

- Down's syndrome is named after Dr. John Langdon Down, who was first to recognise the **medical condition**, in 1866.

- For about every 800 to 1,000 babies born, one will have Down's syndrome.

Fiction

(?) People with Down's syndrome are always happy.

> **WRONG!** They have the same wide range of feelings and moods as everyone else.

(?) People with Down's syndrome all look the same.

> **WRONG!** There are some physical features that some people with Down's syndrome can share. But someone with Down's syndrome will always look more like the members of their family, than like other people with Down's syndrome.

Glossary

cells tiny pieces too small to see, which make up our bodies

coordination ability to move in a skilful, balanced way

develop to change as something grows older

disability illness, injury, or condition that makes it difficult for someone to do the things that other people do

hearing aid device worn inside or next to the ear by people who cannot hear well, in order to help them to hear better

medical condition health problem that a person has for a long time or for life

microscope device that makes very small objects look larger, so people can study them

sign language way of communicating using hands and fingers

Find out more

Books to read

Down's Syndrome (What's it like?), Angela
Royston (Heinemann Library, 2006)

Luke Has Down's Syndrome (Like Me, Like You),
Jillian Powell (Evans Brothers, 2004)

Victoria's Day, Maria de Fatima Compos
(Frances Lincoln Children's Books, 2007)

Websites

**www.downs-syndrome.org.uk/information/i-
have-downs-syndrome.html**
This organization provides help and information
for people who have Down's syndrome, and
their families.

www.ndss.org
Find out lots of information about Down's
syndrome on this website.

Index